SOME BRAINS

A book celebrating neurodiversity

By Nelly Thomas

Illustrations by Cat MacInnes

My brain thinks like this,

IS TIME AN ILLUSION?

WHAT IS FOR BREAKFAST?

And his brain thinks like that.

I see letters FALL from the page,

Leah knows EVERYTHING about the Ice Age.

WOOLLY MAMMOTH

Steppe Bison

Arctic ground squirrel

saiga antelope

Within a single Ice Age are two different phases that can happen alternately multiple times. These two phases are known as 'glacials' and 'interglacials'.

Jan sees numbers **SWIRLING** in circles,

And can even SMELL purple!

If you want a great idea, have ME on your team,
I'll show you an angle, you probably won't see.

(My neuro is not typical – that's why you need me!)

MY NEURO

is not

TYPICAL

what a cool

PART OF ME!

Some people call me
DIFFERENT,

But what does
that mean?

We're ALL different
in some way,
Or YOU would be ME!

I REALLY like quiet,

But my family is LOUD.

Jayden likes
EVERYTHING,

CirroCumulus

Altostratus

StratoCumulus

Cumulus

Cumulonimbus

And Molly
ONLY likes clouds!

My cousin
eats all meals,

I'm more
fastidious.

Jacob only eats
white food,

FOOD i
DO Like

FOOD i
DON'T Like

PopCON PaSTA   evrethingels
RIce   fish
BReD   Chikin
milk   Banana
mash   licheez
yogat   wit pech
Perz   colifloer
cheez   Galic

Alice says,
"Red fruit is hideous!"

My brother has HEAPS of friends,

I like...
1, 2 or 3.

He likes big crowds,
I prefer FAMILY and ME.

Jake uses
iPads and charts.

Some kids are boys,
And others are girls.

I am both ... or neither!
All kids are the joy of the world.

ALL KIDS
are the
JOY
of the
WORLD!

Noise makes me TIRED, And I go home like this...

I groan, "It's so loud and SMELLY! Why can't I give it a miss?!"

I do things at school,
        To help me feel better.

Like
TAPPING
my feet,

Or TRACING over letters.

Once upon a time there a ver

If I look like I'm struggling,
Just give me a minute
...or thirty.

I might need
a rest,

Or my brain will
get HURTY!

ALL KIDS ARE SPECIAL - JUST FOLLOW THEIR HEARTS

Just follow their hearts...

PEOPLE HAVE BEEN DIFFERENT, FOR EVER AND EVER.

That's why we built bridges,
So we can all get together!

My family says,
"We love you just as you are, and in every single way.
Would we ever change you? No way, José!"

(but my name is not José)

LOVE ME
just
AS I
AM

(AND PLEASE DON'T
CALL ME JOSÉ)

GLOSSARY

Neurodiversity

Differences in how brains work. Your brain is like your fingerprint – completely, uniquely yours.

ADHD

The best thing about people with ADHD is that they usually have heaps of energy! They love having fun and doing lots of things. This can make concentrating a bit tricky – they often can't concentrate for long or, they concentrate so hard on one thing they don't notice anything else around them. Kids with ADHD may sometimes find it hard to sit still and listen but they are usually EXCELLENT talkers. ADD is ADHD without the H!

Dyslexia

People with Dyslexia are often very creative and deep thinkers and understand big ideas really easily. They don't usually like "rote learning" or memorising things and have very creative spelling!

Synesthesia

People with Synesthesia have a special super-power – they can sense two or more things AT THE SAME TIME. For example, some people with Synesthesia can *hear* numbers, others can *smell* colours and some can *feel* sounds. There are over 80 types of Synesthesia but neurotypical people can't do any of them.

Aspergers

A place on the Autism Spectrum.

Sensory Processing

Is what the world tells you through your body. People with really excellent sensory processing can hear, see, taste, feel and smell heaps more than everyone else. This can mean the bin will be VERY SMELLY AND GROSS but can also mean that they can smell a beautiful rose down the street. Lights might HURT THEIR EYES but they can see wind! People with really high sensory processing can teach us so much about the world, but they also need a space where they can relax and recover from all that information.

Echolalia

Lots of Autistic kids have an amazing ability to memorise words, songs, phrases and lines from movies. They sometimes use these in conversations with other people or, just to help them feel better.

Perseveration

This basically means when you get stuck on one idea and don't want to stop talking or thinking about it. It is usually a VERY COOL idea but if you stay with it all the time, you won't learn new cool ideas. There are ways adults can help you with perseveration – as long as they are kind and patient.

Dyspraxia

People with dyspraxia have a brain that is very busy doing lots of thinking and sometimes forgets to help the body to move easily. This means Dyspraxic people can be a bit clumsy and they may talk a little bit differently. While neurotypical brains are using up all their energy telling their body how to jump, Dyspraxic brains are doing interesting things like thinking about the world of ideas.

AUTISM

People with a special brain that gives them very cool talents and abilities

THIS *MAY* OR *MAY NOT* INCLUDE ONE OR ALL OF THE FOLLOWING:

- Extra strong smell, sight, touch, hearing or taste.

- A wonderfully sensitive heart that feels *a huge amount* – often making them great artists or friends.

- An ability to focus for a long time on a task – this can sometimes make them great with jobs that need a lot of concentration or repetition. Or not! It all depends on YOU.

- An ability to see patterns – some of the best scientists and mathematicians in history have been Autistic.

- Self-sufficiency – meaning they don't need lots of other people to make them feel happy. Did you know lots of people can't even feel happy unless they're surrounded by others? How exhausting!

- Stimming – the ability to soothe themselves with repetitive behaviours when they get overwhelmed.

- Honesty – many people on the Autism Spectrum are very honest and direct. This is super cool because we need more honesty in the world!

Some people on the Autism Spectrum find other people a bit hard to understand. This is because neurotypical people use ways of communicating that are a bit weird. This can be worked out with help for both of them.

People with Autism may also need a bit more time to do things, but if everyone around them is patient, it is ok!